Sophocles

Electra

Translation by David Bolton

Published by Lulu Books

2019

Copyright by David Bolton

ISBN 978-0-244-52448-7

Terms for the performance of this play may be obtained from
David Bolton at dgbolton0@gmail.com.

All translations in this edition, including the introductory sections (unless
specifically attributed) are by David Bolton.

Colour: #004126

Contents

The background to *Electra*

The curse on the Pelopid dynasty
The mythological founder of the dynasty of which Agamemnon
was a member was Pelops, the son of Tantalus, himself the son of
Zeus, the king of the Olympian gods.
Pindar (*1st Olympian Ode*) recounts that Pelops wanted to marry
Hippodamia, daughter of King Oenomaüs of Pisa in Elis. The king
had already killed thirteen suitors as he delayed his daughter's
marriage. Pelops successfully asked the god Poseidon for help and
received from him a golden chariot and untiring winged horses.
The race between Oenomaüs and a would-be suitor carried the
penalty of death for the loser: Pelops won his race, killed
Oenomaüs and married Hippodamia.
The chorus in *Electra* (*epode of the first choral song [504]*) sing
of Pelops having bribed Oenomaüs' charioteer, Myrtilus, to
sabotage Oenomaüs' chariot; and that after winning, Pelops killed
Myrtilus also, by throwing him into the sea; Myrtilus, as he
drowned, placed a curse on Pelops and his successors and:

"There never has
from Pelops' house been cleansed
that lamentable shame".

The feud between Atreus and Thyestes
Pelops and Hippodamia had three sons, Alcathoüs, Atreus and
Thyestes. These three murdered their half-brother Chrysippus,
after which they fled Pisa: Atreus and Thyestes went to Mycenae,
where Atreus became king, eventually driving out Thyestes.
Most versions of the story maintain that Thyestes brought up
Pleisthenes, Atreus' son by his first marriage to Aërope, as his
own, and sent him to kill Atreus, but that Atreus failed to
recognize his son and killed him in the ensuing fight.
Atreus pretended to offer reconciliation to Thyestes and invited
him to a banquet. He had in fact killed at least one son of
Thyestes, in revenge for the death of Pleisthenes, and cooked and
served the son(s) at the banquet. Thyestes was horrified and fled.

7

Atreus later made a second marriage to Pelopia, who, unknown to him, was already pregnant by her father Thyestes. The child born was Aegisthus.

Atreus, believing him to be his own son, sent Aegisthus to murder Thyestes; but thanks to his father's sword given to Aegisthus by Pelopia, Aegisthus and Thyestes recognized each other as father and son and together went on to kill Atreus and seize the throne of Mycenae.

Agamemnon and Menelaüs

Agamemnon and Menelaüs were sons of Atreus by his first marriage to Hippodamia. They were driven from Mycenae on the death of Atreus and fled to Tyndareüs, king of Sparta.

Agamemnon married Clytemnestra, and Menelaüs married Helen, both daughters of Tyndareüs.

Menelaüs succeeded Tyndareüs as king of Sparta. The abduction of Helen by Paris led to the Trojan War.

Homer's account

Homer says little of Pelops and his descendants up until this time.

There is no mention of Myrtilus' curse; nor is there mention of the feud between Atreus and Thyestes.

Homer does, however, describe Pelops as a 'driver of horses' and describes at least something of the changes in power outlined above in the following passage, in which he also implies that Agamemnon recovered Mycenae on the death of Thyestes:

"King Agamemnon stood up, holding a sceptre which Hephaestus had toiled to make. Hephaestus gave it to Lord Zeus, son of Cronus. Then Zeus gave it to his messenger *(Hermes)*, the slayer of Argus. Lord Hermes gave it to Pelops the driver of horses. Pelops gave it to Atreus the ruler of his people. But Atreus died and left it to Thyestes, rich in lambs; and Thyestes then left it to Agamemnon to bear and to rule over many islands and the whole of Argos." (*Iliad II 100 – 108*).

Agamemnon was certainly established at Mycenae at the outset of the Trojan War.

Included in the 'Catalogue of Ships' in *Iliad II* were:

"Those who held Mycenae, a well-built citadel, wealthy Corinth and well-built Cleonae; those who lived in Orneae and lovely Araethyrea and Sicyon where Adrestus was the first king; those who held Hyperesië and lofty Gonoëssa and Pellenë; those who lived around Aegium, along the whole Aegialus shoreline and around broad Helicë: of their one hundred ships, King Agamemnon, son of Atreus, was the commander."
(*Iliad II 569 – 577*)

During the Trojan War, Agamemnon lists his children:

"...Orestes, who is my beloved son and is being brought up in much abundance. There are three daughters in my well-built halls, Chrysothemis, Laodicë, and Iphianassa..." (*Iliad IX 142 – 145*)

Nestor, king of Pylos, speaking to Telemachus, Odysseus' son:

"For, he *(Aegisthus)* planned a major undertaking. Whilst we sat idly there *(in Troy)* enduring many hardships, he, free of care, in a secluded part of horse-grazed Argos, set about using his charm on Agamemnon's wife. But in fact, at first, goodly Clytemnestra would have nothing to do with his shameful plan, since she employed good sense. With her was a bard whom the son of Atreus had instructed, when he set out for Troy, to watch over his wife. But when the Fates decreed that she should be conquered, he took the bard to a desert island, leaving him as carrion and prey for the birds, and, as a willing man, took the willing woman to his home. He burnt many meaty thigh bones on the holy altars of the gods and hung up many offerings – of robes and gold, having accomplished a major undertaking beyond anything he had hoped for before." (*Odyssey III 261 – 275*)

The immortal seer Proteus tells Menelaüs of Agamemnon's homecoming after the end of the Trojan War:

"But when he *(Agamemnon)* was about to reach the steep-sided Cape Malea, a storm seized him and bore him, groaning deeply, over the fish-filled sea to the border of the country where Thyestes used to have his home, but where then lived Thyestes' son,

Aegisthus. Eventually, there appeared an opportunity for a safe homecoming, when the gods changed the wind back to fair; and they reached home. In truth, he rejoiced as he came to his native land, and he kissed the earth of his home as he touched it. And he wept many warm tears when he joyfully saw the land. But, from a watchtower a watchman saw him. The crafty Aegisthus had taken and placed the man there, and had promised him pay of two talents. This man had kept watch for a year lest he should arrive unseen and think of making an attack; and now he went to give his news to the home of the ruler of his people. Immediately, Aegisthus laid a cunning trap: He selected twenty of the best men of the people and set them in an ambush; elsewhere, he ordered a banquet to be prepared. He himself went with horses and chariots to invite Agamemnon, the ruler of his people, although inwardly thinking shameful thoughts. He led inland a man who was unaware of his doom, and, having dined him, killed him, as one might slaughter an ox in a manger. None of the followers of the son of Atreus survived, nor any of Aegisthus: they were all killed in the Great Hall." (*Odyssey IV 514 – 537*)

Odysseus meets the soul of Agamemnon in the underworld and the soul tells him of Agamemnon's death:
"Son of Laërtes, Zeus-inspired Odysseus of many counsels, Poseidon did not kill me in my ships by raising the melancholy breath of troublesome winds, nor did hostile men slaughter me on the dry land, but Aegisthus prepared my death and doom and killed me with the help of my murderous wife, having called me inside and given me dinner, as one might slaughter an ox in a manger. Thus I died a most lamentable death. All around, my companions were killed in turn like the white-tusked swine of a wealthy and powerful man for a wedding or banquet or magnificent feast. You have by now witnessed the deaths of many men, killed in single combat or in the turmoil of battle, but you would have felt the greatest of horror, had you seen us lying in the Great Hall amongst the wine jugs and laden tables and the whole floor running with blood. Then I heard the most piteous voice of Priam's daughter, Cassandra, whom crafty Clytemnestra killed at

my side. I, dying on the ground, raised my arms to fend off her sword. But she, shameless, walked away, and though I was on my way to Hades, did not lift her hand to shut my eyes or close my mouth. There can, therefore, be no more terrible and shameless woman than she who was minded to do such deeds. And how shameful a deed that woman planned when she won death for her lawfully-wedded husband. In truth, I thought I would be welcomed by my children and household when I returned home; but she, skilled in such base deceit, has poured shame on herself and on all women hereafter, even any who is diligent."
(*Odyssey XI 405 – 434*)

Nestor's explanation to Telemachus continues:
"At this time, Aegisthus hatched his baneful plans at home. Having killed the son of Atreus, he ruled golden Mycenae for seven years and suppressed the people. But in the eighth year, – bad for him – the goodly Orestes came back from Athens and killed the usurper, the crafty Aegisthus, who had murdered his illustrious father. Indeed, having killed him, he held a feast for the people of Argos at the funeral of his hated mother and the cowardly Aegisthus." (*Odyssey III 303 – 310*)

Goddess Athene counsels Telemachus, Odysseus' son, to take action against his mother's suitors and speaks of Orestes' renown:
"Rack your brains as to how you can kill the suitors in these halls – whether by stealth or in open fight. You must not act as a child since you are no longer of that age. Or have you not heard of the renown which goodly Orestes has earned from all men by killing the usurper, the crafty Aegisthus, who murdered his illustrious father?..." (*Odyssey I 294 – 300*)

Events on Olympus:
"All the other gods thronged the halls of Olympian Zeus; and the father of men and of gods addressed them. He had been recalling to mind the noble Aegisthus, whom Agamemnon's son, the renowned Orestes, had killed. With him in mind, he addressed the immortals:

"'Oh dear, how mortals now do blame the gods: they say their ills come from us. But they themselves suffer pain beyond their due by their own recklessness. Take Aegisthus for example. He, beyond his due, married the lawful wife of the son of Atreus whom he had killed on his return home, knowing this would be his complete ruin. After all, we had told him – we sent Hermes, the keen-eyed slayer of Argus, – not to kill him and not to seek his wife as a bride. For, Orestes would avenge the son of Atreus as soon as he grew up and had a desire for his homeland. That is what Hermes said but, in spite of being right, he could not dissuade Aegisthus from his plans, and he has now paid the full price for all his deeds'." (*Odyssey I 26 – 43*)

From the above extracts of the Homeric poems, certain points of interest arise:

Agamemnon led the expedition as a whole, but his immediate leadership (identified by the ships he commanded) extended over Mycenae, the Argolis to the north west of Mycenae, and Achaea. The city of Argos and the Argolis to the east of Argos, including the island of Aegina were under the command of Diomedes, together with Sthenelus and Euryalus.

Homer makes no mention of Agamemnon's daughter Iphigenia. There was a tradition, however, that at Aulis, as the Greeks were attempting to sail off to Troy under the leadership of Agamemnon, the goddess Artemis was offended, apparently by the killing of a stag in her sacred precinct. She stayed the winds and demanded the sacrifice of Agamemnon's daughter, Iphigenia. In spite of not being mentioned by Homer, this tradition became well established and is the subject of Euripides' *Iphigenia at Aulis*. Revenge for this death gives Clytemnestra a motive for the killing of Agamemnon: Clytemnestra puts this motive forward as a justification in *Electra*.

Although some traditions identify Iphigenia with Iphianassa, *Electra* refers to the unnamed Iphigenia sacrificed at Aulis and also to Iphianassa, as a different daughter alive at the time of the action of the play.

Homer names Laodicë as one of Agamemnon's daughters. In later traditions, Laodicë became identified with Electra, as in *Electra*.

Homer relates that Agamemnon brought King Priam's daughter Cassandra home with him to Mycenae: and that Clytemnestra herself killed Cassandra. The relationship between Agamemnon and Cassandra is not mentioned in *Electra*.

The murder of Agamemnon and subsequent revenge exacted by Orestes is dealt with by Homer in the *Odyssey* but not in the *Iliad*. Neither of these events had taken place at the time of the action of the *Iliad*. The principle purpose of introducing the story into the *Odyssey* is to draw a parallel between Orestes' killing his mother's suitor and the potential for Telemachus to drive out the suitors besetting his own mother. Both Athene and Nestor point to the renown Orestes has won for killing Aegisthus. Orestes' killing Clytemnestra has no relevance to Telemachus in the *Odyssey*, since Telemachus had certainly no reason to kill Penelope, who remained constant to her husband Odysseus throughout. It is not surprising, therefore, that the *Odyssey* concentrates on Orestes' killing of Aegisthus and the renown he won from this. Even in the *Odyssey*, however, it can be inferred that Orestes also killed Clytemnestra from the fact that it is reported that he held a feast at the joint funerals of Aegisthus and Clytemnestra. Clytemnestra is described as 'hated', and clearly died at the same time as Aegisthus. Since Aegisthus' was a violent death, it is not unreasonable in the circumstances to suppose Clytemnestra's was also.

Sophocles portrays Orestes as taking advice from the Delphic Oracle, the seat of Apollo, about the action to take against Aegisthus and Clytemnestra. This tradition was also followed by both Aeschylus and Euripides, but is not found in Homer. Homer, as quoted above, has Orestes returning to Mycenae from Athens rather than from Delphi or nearby Crisa.

Whilst Homer speaks of Orestes' renown, the pursuit of Orestes by the Furies, goddesses of vengeance, who were roused by the killing of a mother by her son, is not mentioned in Homer. Nor is it even alluded to in *Electra*.

Orestes and the Delphic Oracle
Homer does not speak of Orestes' consulting the Delphic oracle.
Yet there are references to the Oracle in Homer:

The bard in the court of King Alcinoüs sings of the quarrel between Odysseus and Achilles:
"But Agamemnon, king of men, was delighted that the leaders of the Achaeans were quarrelling. For thus had Phoebus Apollo prophesied to him in sacred Pytho, when he had crossed the stone threshold to consult the oracle. For, then the beginning of suffering was being unleashed on the Trojans and the Danaäns through the counsels of great Zeus." (*Odyssey VIII 77 – 82*)

Achilles, beginning his sulk in his tent, says:
"There is nothing worth my life – not as much as they say the great city Troy possessed earlier in times of peace before the sons of the Achaeans arrived, nor as much as the stone threshold of the archer Phoebus Apollo at rocky Pytho keeps stored inside."
(*Iliad IX 401 – 405*)

Pytho is the earlier name for Delphi: In the 'Catalogue of ships':
"Schedius and Epistrophus …led the Phocians, who held …rocky Pytho, rich Crisa…" (*from Iliad II 517 – 520*)

Archaeological evidence suggests that Pytho was inhabited from Mycenaean times and that it had religious, possibly oracular, significance. Aeschylus in *Eumenides* says that it belonged to Earth and Themis; and the later sanctuary containing the circular temple of Athena Pronaia is thought to have been the site of an earlier practice of the cult of the Earth goddess[1].

The coming of Apollo, that is, the establishment of Delphi as the site of the temple and oracle of Apollo, is associated with the time of Greek colonization in the eighth century BC; Apollo is said to have taken over the place by killing the Python, a dragon, which dwelt there. The Pythian (or Delphic) games are considered to have been first held in 582 BC.

The time of the composition of the *Iliad* and *Odyssey* is problematic. The poems represent an oral tradition and may have been developed and handed down over a considerable period. The poems appear to have been in existence by the mid eighth century BC since references to them are found in quotations dating from that period. The poems were not consolidated into an agreed format until later.

There is therefore no inconsistency in the eighth century seeing both the establishment of Apollo at Pytho/Delphi and a late formulation of the Homeric poems. The fact that Homer refers to 'Pytho' rather than 'Delphi' may be indicative of the transitions taking place at the time. If development of the Homeric poems began much earlier than the eighth century, the references to Apollo at Pytho may be indicative late versions of the poems.

If, however, the view is correct that in Mycenaean times Pytho was associated with the Earth goddess rather than Apollo, then references in Homer to Apollo at Pytho are anachronistic. The Mycenaean period appears to have come to an end not long after 1200 BC, over four hundred years earlier than an eighth century introduction of Apollo to Pytho. The Pedagogue's story in *Electra* of Orestes competing in the Pythian (or Delphic) Games is an even greater anachronism.

---

[1] For discussions about the development of Delphi see eg. *Delphi*, Anna Marandi, *The Peloponnese*, by Karpodini-Dimitriadi and *The Pelican History of Greece*, A.R. Burn.

15

Delphi came to give advice on a range of political, religious and moral issues. In the seventh century BC, it was the chief means in obtaining absolution from blood-guilt. It was presumably in this context that the story of Orestes' visiting the oracle arose.

Orestes and the Furies

The Furies, known also as 'Erinyes' and euphemistically as 'Eumenides' ('Kindly Ones'), were goddesses of vengeance. Hesiod says they were the daughters of the Earth goddess Gaia. They inhabited the Underworld but rose to Earth to pursue the guilty, being particularly associated with blood-guilt, and, in Orestes' case, the killing of his own mother.

In Aeschylus' trilogy, the *Oresteia*, Orestes follows Apollo's commands in killing his mother. He is pursued by the Furies, but returns to Delphi to take refuge. Acting on Apollo's further instructions, he goes to Athens to face trial at the court of the Areopagus. The jury was equally divided; but Athene gave a casting vote to acquit. The Furies were placated and given a cult in which they were called the 'Eumenides'.

In Euripides' play *Iphigenia among the Taurians*, after the acquittal, some Furies remained unappeased. Orestes returned to Delphi again; Apollo commanded him to go to the land of the Taurians and to bring back the statue of Artemis and establish it on Athenian land. This he did successfully.

In the plays, therefore, of Aeschylus, Euripides and Sophocles, Apollo is shown to become the arbiter of blood-guilt: indeed he prescribes the killing of Aegisthus and Clytemnestra. Perhaps the reason for the non-appearance of the Furies in *Electra*, was the emphasis Sophocles wished to place on the supremacy of Olympian Apollo over the chthonic Furies: the supremacy of the justice associated with Delphic Apollo over the policy of revenge pursued by the Furies.

Orestes and Iphigenia

The Temple of Artemis, in the region of what is now Sevastopol in the Crimea, is the scene for Euripides' *Iphigenia among the Taurians*. Orestes, accompanied by Pylades, goes at the command of Apollo to the land of the Taurians to bring the image of Artemis from her temple there to Athens, where a new temple is to be established at nearby Brauron. Orestes recognized Artemis' priestess as Iphigenia: Artemis had in fact substituted a deer at the Iphigenia's sacrifice and had spirited her to the land of the Taurians to be the priestess of her temple there. Iphigenia returned with Orestes to become the priestess of the new temple at Brauron. Even after his trial at Athens, Orestes had continued to be pursued by some of the Furies. But after his establishment of the Temple of Artemis at Brauron, the Furies are appeased.

The date of composition of Electra
Sophocles died in 406/5 BC and produced plays to the end of his life. Stylistic reasons suggest *Electra* is one of his later plays, no earlier than 420 BC.

Mycenae

In the opening few lines of *Electra*, the Pedagogue, standing outside the palace of Mycenae, says "This land is the ancient Argos you used to long for, the grove of the maddened daughter of Inachus". The grove of Inachus refers to the fertile plain of the River Inachus which flows between the cities of Argos and Mycenae. In the Pedagogue's speech, then, 'Argos' refers to the land around Argos and not to the city itself.

However, when the Pedagogue points out various well-known places, Sophocles presents Mycenae as containing the Temple of Hera and the sanctuary of Apollo Lyceüs.

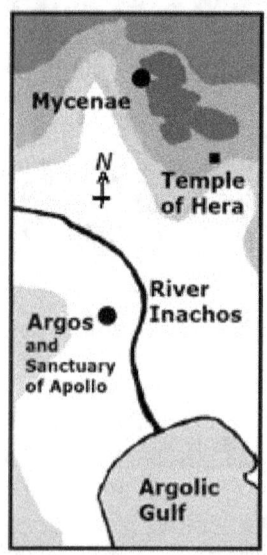

See the front cover for the view from Mycenae towards Argos and the Argolic Gulf.

The sanctuary of Apollo Lyceüs in fact stood outside the *agora* (civic and religious centre) of the city of Argos (and would not even have been immediately visible from Mycenae, which is five or six miles to the north). The famous Temple of Hera stood on a hillside N.E. of Argos and two miles S.E. of Mycenae (from which, also, it would not have been visible because of intervening hills). Neither temple, as known to Sophocles' audience, was of Mycenean construction.

The palace of Mycenae: *megaron* and courtyard

A plan of the *megaron* (Great Hall) and courtyard of the palace complex is set out below. The palace complex sits on high ground within Mycenae. The *megaron* consists of a porch, vestibule and main hall. In the centre of the hall is a hearth. Entrance to the vestibule from the porch would have been secured by doors (and perhaps also from the vestibule to the main hall). The overall length of the *megaron* itself is about 25m. The porch roof is supported by two columns. Four columns around the hearth support a raised area of roof, allowing smoke to leave and light to enter. Columns are Minoan in style.

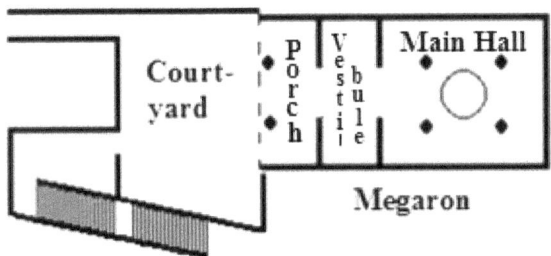

In front of the porch is a courtyard, rather wider than the *megaron* and about half its length. The *megaron* lies broadly west-east, with the courtyard to the west. Access to the courtyard was by a corridor to the north-west corner, or from the top of about forty steps, rising up from east to west to the south-west.

In *Electra*, these entrances are through gates; and the porch of the *megaron* holds seated statues of ancestral gods.

Crisa and Delphi

After the murder of Agamemnon, his son Orestes, still a child, was rescued and sent to King Strophius of Phocis, Agamemnon's brother-in-law. Strophius' own son was Pylades. They lived in Crisa, about a mile south-west of Delphi. Orestes had therefore only a short journey to make to consult the oracle at Delphi.

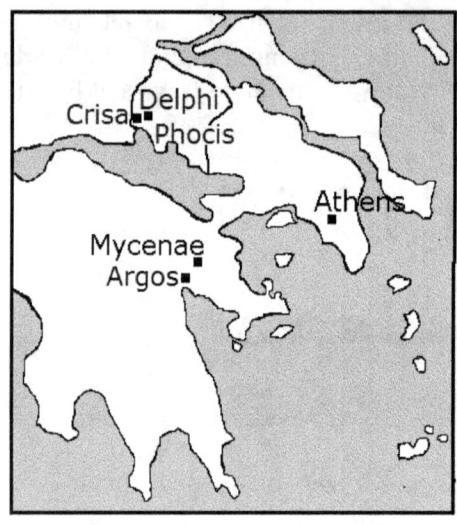

Origins and Life of Sophocles

[The following biography of Sophocles is contained in the various editions of Sophocles, which derive from the thirteenth century and later.]

Sophocles was an Athenian citizen, the son of Sophillus who was neither, as Aristoxenus says, a builder or bronze-smith, nor, as Istrus says, a knife-maker by trade: perhaps he had acquired slave bronze-smiths or builders. For, it is unlikely that someone of such a background would have been considered worthy of a generalship alongside Pericles or Thucydides, the leading men of the city, nor would he have been so completely spared by the comic poets who did not leave even Themistocles unscathed. Also, no credence should be given to Istrus who says that that he was not an Athenian but from Phlius: even if he was originally from Phlius, this is found in no other source other than Istrus. Therefore, Sophocles was an Athenian citizen, from the deme of Colonus; outstanding in his life and poetry, he was well educated, from a wealthy family, and numbered amongst those prominent in public life and who represented of the city.

They say he was born in the second year of the 71st Olympiad [1] in the archonship of Philippus. He was seven years younger than Aeschylus [2] and 24 years older than Euripides [3].

---

[1] The second year of the 71st Olympiad would be 495/4 BC. A consensus of sources would suggest his birth a little earlier, in 496 BC.

[2] Aeschylus is thought to have been born c 525/4 BC: hence, Aeshylus was in fact about 29 years the elder.

[3] Euripides is thought to have been born c 484 BC: hence, Sophocles was in fact about twelve years the elder.

He competed as a boy at wrestling and music, in both of which, according to Istrus, he won victors' crowns. He was taught music by Lamprus, and after the naval battle of Salamis[4], stripped and anointed with oil and accompanying himself on the lyre, he led the singing for the Athenians gathered round the monument of the victory paeans.

He learnt tragedy from Aeschylus. He introduced many innovations to the contests, firstly, owing to his own weakness of voice, abandoning the poet's taking a rôle. For, from times past, the poet had taken a role himself. He also increased the chorus to fifteen members from twelve, and introduced a third actor.

They say that as a player of the cithara he performed on that instrument in *Thamyris* only once, as a result of which he was depicted in the Painted Stoa, playing the cithara.

Satyrus says that he had the idea of the crooked staff, and Istrus says he introduced white boots which both the actors and the chorus wore, that he wrote his plays to suit his actors' qualities, and that he formed a society of educated people to honour the Muses.

In short, the charm of his personality was such that he was held in affection everywhere and by everyone.

He won twenty victories, as says Carystius, and won many second places but never a third.

At the age of 69, the Athenians appointed him general in the war against Anaea, seven years before the Peloponnesian War [5].

He was so devoted to Athens that, though many kings invited him, he was unwilling to leave his native land.

---

[4] The battle of Salamis took place in 480 BC when Sophocles was about sixteen years old.

[5] Anaea overlooks Samos; and it is most likely (from other sources) that Sophocles was elected one of the ten generals and took part in the action against Samos in c 440 BC. He would have been about 56 years old at the time. The Peloponnesian War began in 431 BC.

He held the priesthood of Alcon, which hero's statue...[6] was set up with that of Asclepius alongside that of Chiron, by Iophon, his son, after his death.

Sophocles loved the gods as none other, from what Hieronymus says...[6] about the golden crown. This had been stolen from the Acropolis, and Heracles made a revelation to Sophocles in a dream, saying to hunt for it by going into the...[6] house on the right, where it was hidden. Sophocles displayed it to the deme and received a talent, since that was the advertised reward. Then taking the talent, he established a shrine to Heracles the Revealer.

There are many accounts of a lawsuit against his son Iophon. He had sons Iophon by Nicostratë and Ariston by Theoris of Sicyon. He loved most of all the son of Ariston, also called Sophocles. He once[7] depicted Iophon in a play as envying him and bringing a charge against his father before the clan magistrates that he was demented by old age. They levied a fine on Iophon. And Satyros says that he replied to the charge saying "If I am Sophocles, I am not demented, but if I am demented, I am not Sophocles" and then read from the *Oedipus* [8].

---

[6] There is a lacuna or defective text at this point.

[7] The text here is corrupt. The text suggests an actual lawsuit; but the events leading to the lawsuit appear to be in a play. Different readings of the text suggest Sophocles himself, or Leucon, or Aristophanes was the author of the play.

[8] This play is generally assumed to be *Oedipus Colonus*.

He died [9] in the following way, according to Istrus and Neanthes: Callippides, the actor, came from a production in Opus at the time of the Pitcher-feast and sent him a bunch of grapes; Sophocles put an unripe grape to his mouth and, as a result of old age, choked and died. But Satyrus says he was reading *Antigone* aloud and, near the end, coming upon a long passage, he found in the middle no comma to have a break and for too long read word after word, and lost his life. Others, however, say that after the reading of the play, when he was announced as victor, overcome with joy, he passed away.

He was laid in his ancestral tomb situated on the road to Decelea, eleven stades[10] before the city walls. They say that as a memorial they set up a Siren [11]; others say a bronze Keledon [12]. At this time, the Spartans were building fortifications against the Athenians, but Dionysus stood before Lysander in a dream to permit the man to be placed in the tomb. When Lysander ignored this, Dionysus stood before him a second time with the same instruction. Lysander enquired of fugitives who the dead man was and when he learnt that it was Sophocles, he sent a herald granting the man a burial.

Lobon says that the following was inscribed on the tomb:

> "I hide here Sophocles entombed who took
> first place
> in tragic art, a figure most august."

---

[9] Several sources place his death in the archonship of Callias in 406/5. He mourned the death of Euripides in 406 but was dead by the time of the production of Aristophanes' Frogs in 405.

[10] A stade is equal approximately to one furlong.

[11] Siren: the Sirens were creatures, half bird, half woman who enticed sailors to shipwreck by the beauty of their singing. *Odyssey* (*XII*) tells of their encounter with Odysseus.

[12] Celedon: the Cheledonĕs were mythical songstresses, like the Sirens. They did not, however, have any harmful intent.

Istrus says that the Athenians, on account of the virtue of the man, also passed a decree to make annual sacrifice to him.
He wrote, as Aristophanes says, 130 plays, of which seventeen are spurious.
He competed against Aeschylus, Euripides, Choerilus, Aristias and many others including Iophon, his son.

He spoke of everything in Homeric terms. For, he treated the myths in the footsteps of the poet, and he drew upon the *Odyssey* in many plays. He also took the etymology of 'Odysseus' from Homer's own:

> "I rightly take the name Odysseus
> from my evil woes;
> for many impious men do hold me
> in such odium." [13]

He depicted characters, embellished them and skilfully used contrivances to develop a Homeric charm. On account of this, a certain Ionian said that only Sophocles gained success as a student of Homer. Many others have imitated those before them or those of their own time, but only Sophocles picked from the flower of each. Accordingly, he was spoken of as 'the Bee'. He wrote to combine timing, sweetness, daring and variety.

---

[13] In the *Odyssey*, the person hated was not Odysseus himself, but Autylocus his maternal grandfather:
"Eurycleia placed him in his lap as he finished dinner and spoke as follows: 'Autylocus, it is for you to find a name that we can give to the dear child, since you have prayed for him so much'. Autylocus replied: 'My son-in-law and daughter, give him the name I tell you. I come here being held in odium by many men and women throughout the all-nourishing land; so let his name be Odysseus, signifying this odium'." (*Odyssey XIX 401 – 409*)
The quote of Sophocles is contained in Fragment 965. In the Greek, the etymology hinges on the verb ὀδύσασθαι, 'to hate'. Both ὀδύσασθαι and 'odium', the word used in the translation, are considered to be derived from the Proto-Indo-European root *od- . (*od-: University of Texas at Austin website)

He knew how to time events to a moment, so that from a short half-line or a single phrase he characterized a whole persona. This is the greatest skill of a poet: to show character or suffering.

Aristophanes says "a honeycomb sat on him" and elsewhere "Sophocles had his mouth anointed with honey".

Aristoxenus says that he was the first of the Athenian poets to introduce the Phrygian mode[14] into his songs and intermix the dithyrambic style [15].

[14] Phrygian mode: such music incorporates an octave scale with rising intervals of:
tone, semitone, tone, tone, tone, semitone, tone.
This can be exemplified by the natural notes DEFGABCD.

[15] Dithyramb: originally a song to Bacchus, it came to refer to music in a bombastic style. It apparently derives from the cry of Bacchus when sewn up in his father's thigh: 'rhamma' (ῥάμμα): anything sewn.

Structure of *Electra*

	Lines			Page
Prologue	*1*	-	*120*	33
Lament	*(86*	-	*120)*	36
Entrance of the Chorus			*121*	37
Lament	*121*	-	*250*	37
First episode	*251*	-	*471*	42
First choral song	*472*	-	*515*	48
Second episode	*516*	-	*1057*	49
Lament	*(823*	-	*870)*	58
Second choral song	*1058*	-	*1097*	66
Third episode	*1098*	-	*1383*	67
Recitative	*(1232*	-	*1286)*	72
Third choral song	*1384*	-	*1397*	77
Conclusion	*1398*	-	*1510*	78
Recitative	*(1398*	-	*1441)*	78

Electra

('The Setting of Electra' and Dramatis Personae set out on pages 31 and 32 derive from the transmitted editions of the play.)

The setting of *Electra*

The setting is as follows: His guardian shows Orestes places in Argos. For, as a small child, Electra stole him at the time of her father's murder and gave him to the guardian in fear that they would kill him along with her father. She sent him to Phocis to her father's [....to Anaxibia, his sister] kinsman Strophius [1].

And alternatively:

The old pedagogue in the play, who delivers the Prologue, is the guardian who, having taken Orestes away to Strophius in Phocis, shows him places in Argos. For, the pedagogue, having stolen him as a small child, fled from Argos; and after twenty years [2], he has returned with him to Argos and shows him places in Argos.

The scene of the play is in Argos. The chorus consists of local girls. The pedagogue of Orestes delivers the prologue.

[1] The sentence "She sent him ....Strophius", including the now bracketed "to Anaxibia, his sister", occurs in only one source text. Anaxibia was Agamemnon's sister and wife of Strophius.

[2] Orestes and the Pedagogue returned, according to Homer, in the eighth year after Agamemnon's murder. Orestes was born shortly before the commencement of the Trojan War, which lasted ten years. He may then have been twenty years old on his return, rather than returning twenty years after the murder.

Dramatis Personae[1]

Pedagogue

Orestes

Electra

Chorus of local girls

Chrysothemis

Clytemnestra

Aegisthus

[1] Pedagogue, an old servant; Orestes, son of Agamemnon and Clytemnestra; Electra, daughter of Agamemnon and Clytemnestra; Chorus, of local girls; Chrysothemis, daughter of Agamemnon and Clytemnestra; Clytemnestra, widow of Agamemnon; Aegisthus, usurper of the throne of Argos and Mycenae.
Non-speaking parts:
Retinue of Phocians accompanying Orestes, led by Pylades, son of Strophius, king of Crisa in Phocis; Maid, of Clytemnestra.

The three principle actors take parts as follows: Protagonist: Electra; Deuteragonist: Orestes, Clytemnestra; Tritagonist: Pedagogue, Chrysothemis, Aegisthus.

Electra

Scene: The courtyard in front of the Great Hall of the palace of Mycenae. The large double-doors which lead from the porch of the Great Hall are closed.

Time: The action commences at dawn.

PROLOGUE

(*Enter* Pedagogue, Orestes, *and* Retinue *through a courtyard gate; they have journeyed from Phocis to Mycenae.*)

PEDAGOGUE Son of Agamemnon, that great campaigner of the Trojan War, this is the place you have always been so eager for. Gaze upon it for yourself.

This land is the ancient Argos you used to long for, the grove of the maddened daughter of Inachus;

…here, Orestes, is the sanctuary of Apollo Lyceüs, the wolf-slaying god;

…and on the left, there, the famous Temple of Hera.

This place to which we have journeyed, I may tell you, is golden Mycenae itself, and the death-laden home of the sons of Pelops.

It was from here, after the murder of your father, that I took you from the care of your own sister, kept you safe, and raised you to be the man you are now – to be the avenger of your father's murder.

So now, Orestes, and you, our dearest friend, Pylades, we must decide quickly on a plan of action.

The bright rays of the sun are already rousing the dawn chorus and the dark canopy of stars has left the sky.

Before anyone stirs out of doors, we must be ready. No longer can we rely on delay: it is time for action!

ORESTES Dearest old man, you have always proved yourself a
noble servant. You remind me of a thoroughbred that,
even when it's old, baulks at no danger, but still pricks up
its ears; and you're the same – urging us on, always at the
front!
So then; I'll give you my ideas. Listen closely, and tell me
if you think I've missed anything.
As you know, I went to Delphi to consult the Pythian
Oracle, to learn how I should obtain justice from my
father's murderers; and Phoebus Apollo gave me an
answer: this is what he said:

"No shields or armies; but by guile
do steal, yourself, the rightful deaths".

Those were the instructions. (*to Pedagogue*) So now, you
separate from us and, when there's an opportunity, find
out what is happening inside the palace. And when you
have done so, bring me back a clear report. They will not
recognize you: you will have aged after so long a time and
they will not suspect your grey hair.
You will need a story: how about this…?
Say you are a Phocian, …come from a man called
Phanoteus – he is one of their closest allies. Tell them
…swear to it …that Orestes is dead …killed in an
accident … at the Pythian Games …thrown from a chariot
during a race.
Yes that will do.
We shall go to my father's tomb, as Apollo requires, and
there pour libations and dedicate locks of our hair. We
shall then meet up with you; and we shall bring with us
that bronze urn – there's one, as you know, which lies
hidden in the bushes there; we can use it in our deception,
as we bring them the news which will so please them, that
I am dead, and that my body is cremated and reduced to
ashes in that urn.

What harm could a mere report do when I am in fact safe and about to earn nothing but renown? It seems to me words do no injury which lead to gain. Indeed, I have often seen even wise men said falsely to have died; and when they have returned home again, they have been held in all the greater honour. And it is my boast that, with the help of our story, I shall be all too much alive for my enemies and that my star will continue to shine for a long time yet.

(*raising his hands in prayer*) But now: My own land and the gods who dwell in it! Give me good fortune in my enterprise! And you, my father's house, I have been sent here by the gods to purify you in justice. Do not send me away without honour, but rather with ancient riches as the restorer of my house.

My prayer is said.

(*to Pedagogue*) So now, old man, go, and take care to play your part. We two (*indicating Pylades*) must also be on our way.

The time is upon us and time is the great overseer of all men's works.

(Electra *is heard weeping inside the Great Hall.*)

ELECTRA (*from the Great Hall, off-stage*) Oh! How wretched I feel!

PEDAGOGUE My boy; I'm sure I heard one of the servants in there in tears.

ORESTES Could it be poor Electra? Do you think we could wait a few moments and find out who she is?

PEDAGOGUE Certainly not. Nothing but the commands of Apollo must occupy us now; and it is for you to make a start by pouring libations at your father's tomb. And, I can assure you, we must proceed if we are to win victory and success.

(*Exeunt* Pedagogue *through a courtyard gate, and* Orestes *and* Retinue *through the other courtyard gate*)

(*Enter* Electra *from the Great Hall*)

[Sung lament]

[86]
ELECTRA O holy light
          and air which share this Earth, you hear
          my many songs of grief,
          the many heavy blows
          directed at my blooded breast
          as dark-born night to daytime yields.
          My loathsome bed in a troubled house
          to night-long vigils witness bears,
          as I lament that wretched man,
          my father, whom the God of Death
          did not embrace in *foreign* lands;
          yet *here* my mother and her vile
          Aegisthus, split his head in twain,
          like woodmen wielding blooded axe.
          No grief from anyone but me
          is shown for you, dear father, sent
          to shameful sad, sad death.
          And I shall not
          my anguished mournful weeping cease
          whilst I the twinkling stars
          can see, or yet the day.
          But like the nightingale who slew
          her children, piteously I wail
          at these the doors of father's home.
          O Hades and Persephone,
          O Hermes, you, Goddess Revenge,
          O Furies, children of the gods,
          who see those suffering unjust deaths,
          betrayed in stolen marriage vows,

36

O come! Give help! Avenge the death
of father now.
And send my brother safe to me!
For I no longer have the strength
to counteract such grief!

ENTRANCE OF THE CHORUS

(*Enter* Chorus *through the courtyard gates*)

[Sung lament]

[121]
CHORUS   *[strophe]*

Dear Electra, child ill-born
to mother's taint of wretchedness,
why drink of pain unsatisfied
for Agamemnon, whom by guile
a mother trapped, an evil hand
betrayed? Let him, who did this, die,
if gods of Right speak well!

ELECTRA

Noble children, noble!
Comfort for my grief you bring;
I understand all that you say;
but still unwilling I remain
to cast off grief at father's death.
But you who come
exchanging every friendship's grace,
do let me weep,
Oh! Oh! I pray you.

CHORUS   *[antistrophe]*
    None can bring your father back
    from Hades' all-consuming marsh,
    not for all your tears and prayers.
    From measured ways, now uncontrolled
    you nurse a painful broken heart,
    for which no remedy avails.
    But why desire such pain?

ELECTRA
    Foolish he who soon for-
    gets a parent's pitiable fate.
    My mood befits the nightingale,
    which wails in grief "Itüs, Itüs",
    bewildered bird, Zeus' messenger.
    And Niobë
    all-suffering, you I think a god,
    in rock entombed,
    to weep for ever.

CHORUS   *[strophe]*
    Not to you alone
    of mortals, child, comes grief.
    But yours seems heavy; less is theirs,
    your blood relations', born to be
    as you: Chrysothemis lives well,
    and Iphianassa.
    And then that blessed youth
    laments in hiding, whom
    Mycenae will
    to Zeus' great altars home receive.
    Thus your Orestes will come back!

ELECTRA
Yes, untiring, I await him,
childless, wretched, without husband.
My face is ever wet with tears
in endless doom; forgetful he
of all he suffered, all he learnt.
And what report's but proved untrue?
He may for ever want,
but wanting brings him not to me.

CHORUS   *[antistrophe]*
Courage, courage! Child.
In heaven still the great
Lord Zeus looks down on all and rules;
entrust your tortured rage to him.
Bear not too heavy load of hate,
nor yet forget. For time's
an easy-going god,
and neither he, who lives
at ox-grazed Crisa, e'er
forgetful is –
the son of Agamemnon –, nor
the god that rules by Acheron's shore.

ELECTRA
So much of life has passed me by
devoid of hope; I lack all strength
who without children pine away.
No husband have I me to guard,
but like some worthless stranger work
to care for father's home
with empty tables, shabby clothes.

CHORUS   *[strophe]*
    Met with cries the coming home of
    Agamemnon; blood-soaked couches
    when the axe-blade struck him down.
    Guile the driver, Lust the killer,
    generating awful forms and
    spectres. Was a God or was a
    man the murderer?

ELECTRA
    O that day above all others
    hateful in its meaning to me!
    O night, O awful weight of pain
    of shameful dinner served!
    My father saw
    unworthy death, two pairs of hands,
    which stole my life,
    betrayed, destroyed.
    O may the Olympian god
    inflict his retribution.
    No glory let reflect on them
    for such a deed as that.

CHORUS   *[antistrophe]*
    Best for you to say no more now.
    Surely you must understand whence
    come your troubles; to destruction
    oh so shameful now you fall as
    ever needless evils crowd; your
    angry soul gives birth to warfare,
    which 'gainst them, the strong, in power,
    contemplate not.

ELECTRA

> Base my deeds from base compulsion.
> Know I all this. Clear, my anger.
> In such danger, no avoidance
> of destruction is there,
> whilst I live still.
> My companions! Who can give a
> word of comfort…
> …who – right thinking?
> Leave me now, so leave me.
> No solution offers.
> Toiling, will I never cease from
> endless lamentation.

CHORUS   *[epode]*

> With goodwill we bid you,
> as a trusted mother might,
> bring not ruin onto ruin.

ELECTRA

> Moderate be when faced with evil?
> Come! Neglect the dead be proper?
> Where is this the way of men?
> May I not by them be honoured
> now or ever; nor if riches
> winning, live amongst them, carefree,
> curbing wings of shrill-toned wailing
> for my father.
>
> If the dead, as earth and nothing,
> shall untended lie,
> whilst *they* in turn
> shall fearless and unpunished live,
> *then* destroyed is shame, and
> lost is man's respect for god.

41

[251]

CHORUS My child, we came to help you as one of ourselves. But
if our words are out of place, do as you will.
We shall always support you.

ELECTRA I am sorry, girls, if I seem excessive in my grief.
Abuse has driven me to behave as I do: so pardon me.
How could a woman of noble birth not act as I do when
she sees such calamities destroying her family, which,
every day and night, I see multiply rather than diminish?
First of all, everything to do with my mother – who bore
me – has become hateful to me. Then, I have to share my
home with my father's murderers: I am ruled by them, I
have to depend on them – and I am deprived by them.
What kind of days do you think I spend when I see
Aegisthus sitting on my father's throne, and when I see
him wearing the same royal clothes as he and pouring
libations to the gods at the hearth where he murdered him,
and when I see their ultimate act of hubris, – that murderer
and that wretched mother of mine sharing my *father's*
bed, if I must call her mother who lives with *him*? She is
brazen enough to live with that polluting criminal, yet she
fears no Avenging Fury. She actually laughs at the deed,
and marks the date on which they tricked and killed my
father, by holding a festival; and every month she
slaughters sheep in offering to her patron gods.
But I, ill-fated, see all this and, in my room, weep and
pine away, and by myself lament at the wicked
celebrations they have named after him. But I cannot
weep as much as my heart would want.
But *she*, that so-called noble lady, pours scorn on me and
says:
"You god-forsaken miserable object, are you the only one
for whom your father is dead? Does no-one else grieve?
May *you* die as well, and may the gods beneath make sure
you have good reason to cry!"

42

Such are her insults ….except when she hears any report that Orestes is coming. Then she stands over me in a rage and shouts:

"You are the cause of all this! You are the one who stole Orestes out of my arms and carried him off! Be sure you will pay for that!"

Such is her abuse; and urging her on nearby is that wonderful bridegroom of hers, that coward, that contaminant, who fights his battles alongside women.

But as I wait – endlessly – for Orestes to come and end my misfortunes, I am dying a sorrowful death. Whilst he is always full of intentions, he has in reality destroyed all my strong – and not so strong – hopes.

In such circumstances, I can show neither common sense nor piety. Rather, when surrounded by evil, it is a matter of necessity to foster evil.

CHORUS Be careful what you say! Is Aegisthus at home…. or is he away?

ELECTRA If he were at home, I would not be standing out here. He is away at the moment.

CHORUS I feel more comfortable talking to you if that is so.

ELECTRA He is away; so you can speak. What do you wish to say?

CHORUS I would like to ask whether you have any news of your brother. Does he say whether he is coming or not? We're eager to know.

ELECTRA He says he is coming. He talks about it but does nothing.

CHORUS A man likes to delay before any great enterprise.

ELECTRA I didn't delay when it came to saving his life.

CHORUS Be confident. He is a noble man and will help those dear to him.

ELECTRA I believe you; otherwise I would not have lived so long.

CHORUS (*as the doors of the Great Hall open*) Say no more now! I see your sister Chrysothemis coming out. She is carrying offerings for the dead.

43

(*Enter* Chrysothemis *from the Great Hall*)

[328]

CHRYSOTHEMIS Sister, what are you talking about out here?
After all this time, have you still not learnt not to cherish
empty hopes?

And yet, I know the extent of my own suffering at present;
indeed, if I could muster the strength, I would tell them
what I think. But now, times are bad and I think it best to
ride the storm and not to appear too active or to rile them.
And I wish you would do the same.

In reality, I agree justice lies not in what I say but as you
see it. But if I am to live in freedom, those in power have
to be listened to.

ELECTRA How awful that you forget your own father – whose
child you are – and care only for her who brought you into
the world. All the warnings you give me come from her.
None of this comes from you.

Now choose one or the other: either live without moral
courage, or show some courage and have no thought for
your present 'friends'.

You have just said that if you could muster the strength,
you would show them how you hated them. But whilst I
do everything I can to avenge father, you offer no
cooperation; in fact, you aim to dissuade me who am at
least doing something. Does this not add cowardice to
your other failings?

Tell me what I would gain if I ceased mourning the dead;
or rather listen to what I have to say. Am I not alive? A
poor life, I know, but a sufficient one. I cause them
trouble in order to honour a dead man – if there is any
appreciation from that quarter.

You tell me you hate them, but whilst you talk about it, in
practice, you live with father's murderers.

I would never give in to them, not even if someone were
to present me with a life as luxurious as yours. You can

44

have your richly set tables and your life flowing with abundance! Just give me enough food not to starve! I have no desire, like you, to be held in their high regard; and, if you had any sense, neither would you. You could be considered the child of the noblest of fathers; but you prefer to be your mother's. And everybody thinks you are evil and a traitor to your dead father and to those dear to you!

CHORUS No angry words in the presence of the gods! Perhaps both of you could learn from this conversation.

(*to Electra*) If you were to listen to what she has to say, she might listen to you in return.

CHRYSOTHEMIS I am quite accustomed, young ladies, to her nonsense.

I would pay it no attention – except that I have heard that something is about to happen which will put an end to her weeping once and for all!

ELECTRA So, what is this terrible news, then? Are matters going to become even worse? I don't care if they do.

CHRYSOTHEMIS I'll tell you what I know.

They are going, if you do not mend your ways and cease your weeping, to send you to some cave deep in the earth, untouched by the rays of the sun, to live there, where you can recite you prayers unheard.

Listen to what I tell you and don't say I didn't warn you. Now, please, be sensible.

ELECTRA Their plans are fully laid?

CHRYSOTHEMIS ...and will be put into effect as soon as Aegisthus returns.

ELECTRA The sooner the better.

CHRYSOTHEMIS My dear sister, why curse yourself?

ELECTRA If those are his plans, let him come!

CHRYSOTHEMIS To what purpose? Have you lost your senses?

ELECTRA So that I can get away from all of you!

CHRYSOTHEMIS But what of your present life?

ELECTRA Oh yes, what a wonderful life that is!

CHRYSOTHEMIS But it could be, if you would only learn common sense…

ELECTRA …by forsaking him who is dear to me.

CHRYSOTHEMIS No, I'm not saying that. Just go along with those in power.

ELECTRA You can do that. But that is not my way.

CHRYSOTHEMIS Well, how brilliant to be ruined through stupidity!

ELECTRA Let me be ruined …if that is the price of retaliation for father.

CHRYSOTHEMIS Father, I know, would forgive you.

ELECTRA Such words are not worthy of you.

CHRYSOTHEMIS Will you not be persuaded?

ELECTRA Certainly not. I am not so empty-headed.

CHRYSOTHEMIS Then I shall be on my way.

ELECTRA Where are you going? And what is that you are carrying?

CHRYSOTHEMIS Mother sent me to make offerings at father's tomb.

ELECTRA What's that?! She …hated him!

CHRYSOTHEMIS "…killed him" is what you usually say.

ELECTRA What has prompted all this, anyway?

CHRYSOTHEMIS Some bad dream, apparently.

ELECTRA O ancestral gods, be with me now!

CHRYSOTHEMIS Her alarm at this dream brings you hope?

ELECTRA It may do: if you would tell me what this dream was.

CHRYSOTHEMIS I only heard a few words about it.

ELECTRA Well, tell me what you know. A few words have often made the difference between life and death.

CHRYSOTHEMIS The word is that she dreamt she met your …and my …father again, as he returned once more to the light of day. He took the sceptre which he used to bear, and which Aegisthus now bears, and planted it by the hearth; and out of it grew a branch full of leaves, which grew so large as to cast a shadow over the whole of Mycenae.

She revealed her dream to the Sun-god and I heard this from someone who was with her at the time.

I know nothing further, except that she has sent me on my errand out of fear of this dream.

But by the gods of our race, I beg you to listen to me and do not give in to stupidity.

ELECTRA Dear sister, on no account make offering of what you carry at father's tomb. It would be improper and unholy to make any offering or pour any libation on behalf of a woman who is his enemy. Either throw them to the winds or bury them in the earth so that they go nowhere near the resting place of our father. They can be treasure laid in store for *her* when *she* dies.

To begin with, if she were not the most shameless of women, she would never think to pour a libation to honour a man she killed, her enemy. Consider whether you think they will be received as loving gifts from her by the corpse of him that was slain with such dishonour, then horribly mutilated, and then, by way of absolution for her, had the blood on her hands wiped off over its head.

By doing that, do you think she washed away the stains of her guilt? She did not!

Throw them away. Instead, cut a lock of hair from your own head, and from me – a small thing, but all I have – take this lock of my neglected hair...and this belt – even though it is rather plain. Give them to him, and beg him on your knees to send us help from below the earth against our enemies, and to send Orestes alive and in strength to trample on our foes, so that for the rest of time we may garland his tomb with richer gifts than ever we can now.

I believe... I truly believe that he has sent her this fearful dream. Whether so or not, sister, do this for yourself, and be of help to me and to that dearest of mortals who lies in Hades, our common father.

CHORUS (*to Chrysothemis*) She speaks with piety. I say to you as a friend, would you not be wise to do as she says?

47

CHRYSOTHEMIS   I will. And duty calls us not to argue but to
act quickly together.
But also, since I am doing as she asks, by the gods, I need
your silence, my friends. If my mother finds out, I shall
surely rue the day!

(*Exit* Chrysothemis *through a courtyard gate.*)

FIRST CHORAL SONG

[472]
CHORUS   *[strophe]*
If I am no wild seer, my child,
nor lacking yet in judgment sound,
there soon will come
great Justice, power in her hands.
A little time: she will be here!
My confidence is risen,
since now from her I hear of these
sweet-sounding dreams.
Your father, Lord of Greece,
does never you forget,
nor does the bronze-cast blade
of the double-headed axe,
which, wielded, cut him down
so shamefully to death.

With many feet and many hands,
will come in hidden ambush laid
the Furies dread.
For, strife from wrongful marriage rose,
which was no marriage, no true bride.
Before, such confidence we've
never, never had;
The portent – now draw near
'gainst those who played a part;
For, man's prophetic power
cannot derive from dreams
nor from the words of god
unless this phantom of
the night brings us success.

[epode]

O strife-worn chariot race
of Pelops, on this land
you placed your curse.
For, Myrtilus did die
by drowning long ago,
from golden chariot flung
by Pelops into the sea,
disgracefully, against his word.
There never has
from Pelops' house been cleansed
that lamentable shame.

SECOND EPISODE

(*Enter* Clytemnestra *and* Maid *from the Great Hall*)

[516]
CLYTEMNESTRA (*to Electra*) Unbridled as usual. It is a pity
    Aegisthus is not here. He would soon put a stop to your
    hanging about out of doors, criticizing your loved ones.

He is away at the moment, and nothing I say has any effect on you.

I know you have a great deal to say to everyone about me: that I rule arrogantly and beyond my rights; that I treat you and your kind with contempt. But *I* am not the contemptuous one: and if I criticize you, it's in response to your repeatedly criticizing me.

Your one excuse is your father: that he died at my hands. At my hands: yes, I know; I do not deny it.

But Justice took him, not I alone. And you would agree with me about that if you had any sense.

That father of yours, whom you insist on weeping for all the time, was the only Greek leader who took it upon himself to sacrifice to the gods his own… kinswoman. He was her father, yes, but his grief was not equal to mine, her mother.

Ah! Tell me this: for whose sake did he sacrifice her? Was it for the Greeks? Is that what you say? He had no right to kill *my* daughter for them! He, rather than his brother Menelaüs, chose to kill – and my daughter: don't you think he should pay me back for that? Did not Menelaüs have two children? Was it not right that they should have died rather than mine? It was their father and mother who were the cause of the expedition in the first place. Or perhaps Hades had some particular desire to feast on my children rather than theirs? Or was it, in reality, that your utterly useless father cared nothing for his children, whilst Menelaüs did care about his? Pathetic actions of a pathetic man without a thought in his head!

My views differ from yours. But I can assure you that the dead girl would agree with me if she had a voice to speak.

So, I am not dispirited at anything that has happened. If you think I'm wrong, consider both sides of the question …and blame those close to you.

ELECTRA You can hardly blame me for criticizing you, having heard what you have just said. But if you will allow me, I

50

will put forward the cases fairly of both my dead father and my dead sister.

CLYTEMNESTRA I *am* allowing you. And if you had always spoken politely, I would have been happy to listen to you.

ELECTRA I say this: you say you killed father. What could be more shameful, whether you acted justly or not?

And I say to you that you did not kill him justly, but out of desire for that evil man you now live with.

Ask the huntress, Artemis, what she was punishing when she becalmed the fleet at Aulis. I will tell you. My father, so I heard, was hunting in the sacred grove of the goddess and as he walked, disturbed a dappled antlered stag and made some boastful comment when he struck and killed it. Artemis was so annoyed at this that she held back the Greeks. She, a goddess, demanded that father in compensation for the stag should sacrifice his own daughter. That is how her sacrifice came about. There was no other way to free the armies either to go home or to go on to Troy. And for this reason he was compelled, in spite of offering much resistance, reluctantly to sacrifice her. It was not for Menelaüs.

And even if, to accept your point of view, he acted as he did because he wanted to help him, ought he really to have died at your hand? By what law? Be careful that you do not establish laws which will rebound on *you* in a way you will repent.

If we take a life for a life, you would be the first to die, if there were any justice.

Make sure you do not make false excuses. Then, please, tell me why you carry on in the most shameful manner of all, sleeping with that murderer, with whom you set out to destroy my father and by whom you now produce children, throwing out your innocent and legitimate children born of a legitimate marriage. How could I agree with that? Are you really saying you are exacting revenge for your daughter? You would not have the nerve! It is no noble act to marry an enemy for the sake of a daughter!

51

I'll say no more. It isn't possible to reason with you: you say to all and sundry that I am bent on saying horrible things about you. Well, as far as I am concerned, you are a despot, not a mother, to us. I lead an awful life, and receive nothing but ill-treatment from you and from him you live with. And that poor boy abroad, who only just managed to escape your clutches, Orestes, also has a harsh life to grind out. You have often accused me of nursing an avenger of your blood-defiled crime! And I would, believe you me, if I could! All right; I've said it. So announce to everyone that I am evil, or, if you prefer it, tiresome or shameless. But, I can tell you, even if I were to practise, I couldn't come close to putting your character to shame!

CHORUS She's breathing fire! Even if she is right, I think she is losing her sense of reason.

CLYTEMNESTRA And what kind of sense of reason do *I* need, to deal with someone like her …so insolent to her mother? And at her age!

(*to Electra*) Have you no sense of shame?!

ELECTRA I have a sense of shame all right …even if I don't seem to to you! *I* know why my behaviour is odd and puts me in a bad light. Your attitude and behaviour simply force me to do as I do.

My behaviour is unworthy? *You* are unworthy!

CLYTEMNESTRA Shameless creature! It is I, then – what I say and do – which make you have too much to say!

ELECTRA You said it, not me! *You* did what you did; and what you did speaks for itself!

CLYTEMNESTRA By lady Artemis, you won't get away with this! Wait till Aegisthus gets home!

ELECTRA Typical! You just get angry! You ask me to say what I think! But then, you just don't listen!

CLYTEMNESTRA Can't you keep quiet and allow me to make my sacrifice in peace, especially since I've allowed you to have your say?

ELECTRA Go on; I want you to; make your sacrifice! Don't let my mouth get in the way! I'm saying no more.

52

(*Electra moves angrily well away from Clytemnestra*)

CLYTEMNESTRA   (*to Maid*) You, Maid, take hold of these
    offerings.
    I wish to say a prayer to my Lord to set me free from fear.
    (*holds her hands in prayer*)
    Lord Apollo my Protector, you have already heard my
    guarded words: I am not amongst friends; nor can I bring
    everything to the light whilst she is near me, lest she with
    spiteful tongue sow false rumour about the city.
    But listen to my prayer.
    Apollo, the apparitions of my two night-time dreams, if
    they foretell good, let them come to fruition; but if bad, let
    them rebound on my enemies. If you are telling me that
    any are plotting to eject me from my present riches, do not
    allow it, but let me live as I do, secure, in the house of the
    sons of Atreus, wielding the royal sceptres, enjoying the
    company of my friends, and living pleasantly with those
    of my children who neither dislike me nor display bitter
    grief.
    This, Apollo Lyceüs, is my prayer. Receive it graciously
    and grant to all of us what I ask. Although I am silent on
    other matters, I am sure you, as a god, will understand,
    since those descended from Zeus see all.

(*Enter* Pedagogue *through a courtyard gate*)

[660]
PEDAGOGUE   Ladies, could you please tell me if this is the
    home of the ruler Aegisthus?
CHORUS It is; you have come to the right place.
PEDAGOGUE   (*to Chorus, indicating Clytemnestra*) And am I
    right in supposing that that lady is his wife? She has the
    appearance of a ruler's wife.
CHORUS You are correct; that is she.

53

PEDAGOGUE   Good day, my Lady. I bring good news to you
      …and to Aegisthus …from a friend.
CLYTEMNESTRA I welcome the omen! But first, please tell me
      who sent you.
PEDAGOGUE Phanoteus, the Phocian. He considers his message
      of great importance.
CLYTEMNESTRA My good man, tell me what he has to say. He
      is a good friend, I know. His news will also be good.
PEDAGOGUE There has been a death …in a word …Orestes.
ELECTRA Oh no! I too am dead today!
CLYTEMNESTRA   (to Pedagogue) What's that?! What's that
      you say?! Pay no attention to her.
PEDAGOGUE As I said …Orestes is dead.
ELECTRA   I may as well be dead also!
CLYTEMNESTRA   (to Electra) You; go away and find
      something to do. (to Pedagogue, as Electra moves to
      stand by one of the gates at the entrance to the courtyard)
      Tell me truly how it happened. How did he die?
PEDAGOGUE I will tell you everything that happened.
      He went to take part in the games, famous throughout
      Greece, held at Delphi. And when the heralds announced
      the first race, he entered. He looked fit and impressive:
      everyone thought so. He ran the race in a manner expected
      of his physique and ability: he won, and carried off the
      victor's prize. To cut a long story short, I never saw a man
      give such a powerful display. Believe me, every race the
      heralds announced, he won; and he received each prize
      with the announcement "An Argive, by name Orestes, son
      of the famous Agamemnon, sometime leader of the
      Greeks".
      And so it went on.
      But when a god takes hold, not even the strongest can
      escape.
      At sunrise on another day, the chariot races were held, and
      he entered along with many other charioteers. One was
      Achaean, one was from Sparta, and two Libyans, all with
      their yoked chariots. A fifth had Thessalian horses. A

sixth was from Aetolia with chestnut colts. A seventh was from Magnesia and an eighth, with white horses, was of the Aenian race. A ninth was from Athens, the city founded by the gods. Then there was a Boeotian riding the tenth chariot. They lined themselves up ready in the order drawn by lot by the judges; and when the trumpet sounded …they were off! Together, they shook their reins to urge on their horses. The whole track was filled with the rattling clatter of the chariots. A cloud of dust was thrown up; and as they crowded together, no-one spared the whip as each tried to overtake the wheels of those in front and on past the whinnying horses. Foam clung to the horses' mouths as their hot breath burst onto the charioteers' backs and the turning wheels.

To begin with, all the chariots stayed upright, but then the horses of the Aenian went out of control, and as they turned at the end of the sixth lap to start the seventh, they crashed headlong into the Libyan horses. This caused each chariot to collide with the next, until the whole racecourse was strewn with smashed chariots. But the wily Athenian driver drew his horses aside and held them back, allowing the surge of horses to crash together in the middle. And also, at the back, with the last horses, drove Orestes, pinning his hopes on a final sprint. When he saw that the Athenian was the only other left in the race, he gave a piercing shout into his horses' ears and pursued his rival. The two drew level; now one pair, now the other pushed their heads in front. Orestes, when he came to each turning point, always grazed it with his wheel, and, letting the right-hand horse run on, reined in the left. He completed all the laps safely, keeping his chariot out of trouble and upright. Then, …he accidentally lost hold of the left rein of the inside horse as it was turning and he crashed into the tall turning post. The axel shattered, and he was pulled from the rails and became entangled in the reins. His horses, as he fell, pulled apart across the track. The crowd saw him dragged out of his chariot, and there

55

was a loud gasp and cries of shock for the young man who had performed so well but had met with such an accident. He was pulled head over heels to the ground, and after the other charioteers, with some difficulty, had pulled up their horses, they managed to free him from the reins; but he was so covered in blood that not even a friend would have recognized his dead body.

His remains ...were burnt on a pyre soon after. Some Phocians were chosen, to bring his once fine body, now feeble dust, in a bronze urn, here to be placed in a tomb in his ancestral homeland.

Such is my news, painful to relate, and for those who saw it happen, as we saw it, as shocking a sight as any I have ever witnessed.

CHORUS Oh no! And the line of the ancient family is at an end, so it seems.

CLYTEMNESTRA O Zeus, shall I say this news is fortunate ...or awful ...whilst yet to my advantage? It grieves me to think that I save my own life at such a dreadful cost.

PEDAGOGUE What have I said to cause you such despondency?

CLYTEMNESTRA Childbearing is a terrible thing. Even a woman who is ill-used cannot feel hatred for one she has borne.

PEDAGOGUE Perhaps then my journey is in vain.

CLYTEMNESTRA No, not in vain; how could you say 'in vain'? ...if you bring proof, that is, of the death of this man that was born of my soul but who was taken from my breast and care and estranged from me, an exile.

From the day he went away, he never saw me again. But he accuses me of murdering his father and has made dreadful threats against me. As a result, sweet sleep has soothed me neither night nor day and the threat of his imminent arrival drives me nearly to death.

But now...; today I have gained my freedom from fear of *her* (*indicating Electra*) and of that man. *She* had a greater hold on me since she lived here, incessantly draining my life's blood; ...but *now*, free of her threats, I can pass my days in peace.

ELECTRA   Oh... *Now*, Orestes, as well as your misfortune, I must lament that, even in death, you are still being abused by our mother! Can that be right?

CLYTEMNESTRA   You're not right. But he's all right as he is.

ELECTRA   Nemesis of the dead man, listen to this!

CLYTEMNESTRA   Nemesis has heard all she wants to hear and has acted appropriately!

ELECTRA   Insolent woman ...now that fortune is with you!

CLYTEMNESTRA   Isn't it time you and Orestes stopped all this?

ELECTRA   Time to stop..?! We are stopped!

CLYTEMNESTRA   (*to Pedagogue, sarcastically*) My good man, you really would do us a valuable service if you could put a stop to her wild tongue.

PEDAGOGUE   I think, in fact, if all is well, I shall be on my way...

CLYTEMNESTRA   No, no; I couldn't just let you leave; I owe it to the man who sent you.... Come inside, and leave her out here to bemoan her situation and that of her friends.

(*Exeunt* Clytemnestra, Pedagogue *and* Maid *into the Great Hall*)

ELECTRA   Do you think the wretched woman sheds pitiful tears at the loss of her dead son, as if she were grieving and in pain? ...whilst laughing at his passing away. Oh dear!

Dearest Orestes, in dying, you have killed me also. Your leaving us has torn from my heart the only hope that still remained ...that you would come sometime, alive, to avenge father and poor me. Where should I go now? ...now that I am alone ...without you or father. I shall be a slave again ...amongst enemies, amongst our father's killers. Will all be well with me? Well, I shall definitely never ever again live in *there*. But rather, I shall allow myself to sink to the ground here, by this gate, and live out my life without friends. Those in there can deal with

57

me as they like, if I am a nuisance to them. Death would
be a favour to me, life a burden. I have no desire to live.

[Sung lament]

[823]
CHORUS   *[strophe]*
>   Where the thunderbolts of Zeus, or
>   where the blazing Sun-god? Do they
>   watch on us, unmoved?
ELECTRA
>   (*weeping*) Aíaiaí...
CHORUS
>   ...You weep still?
ELECTRA
>   Dead; he's dead!...
CHORUS
>   ...But are we sure?
ELECTRA
>   You kill me!...
CHORUS
>   ...We?
ELECTRA
>   If you do try to give me hope
>   of those so clearly dead and gone,
>   then me, who pine away,
>   you simply trample down.

CHORUS   *[antistrophe]*
>   Yet, was once Lord Amphiaraüs,
>   trapped by woman's golden snare, but
>   now beneath the earth...
ELECTRA
>   Aíaiaí...
CHORUS
>   ...alive rules.

58

ELECTRA
> Yes...

CHORUS
> ...a deadly woman, then...

ELECTRA
> ...had killed him...

CHORUS
> ...Yes.

ELECTRA
> I know; appeared then an
> avenger for his plight.
> None such for me. Who lived,
> has now been snatched in death.

CHORUS   *[strophe]*
> What wretched, sorry thoughts you have.

ELECTRA
> I *know* I do – know all too well
> – since month on month I lead
> a life of awful woe.

CHORUS
> We understand your grief.

ELECTRA
> No longer, never, now
> suggest to me that there...

CHORUS
> Think what you say!

ELECTRA
> ...that there is hope
> of help from any kin of mine.

CHORUS   *[antistrophe]*
> For every mortal, fate is set.

ELECTRA
> To die whilst racing horses, though,
> entangled in his reins,
> as did this poor young man.

59

CHORUS
    So unexpected, this.
ELECTRA
    To think, a stranger he,
    not in these arms of mine…
CHORUS
    Aiaíai…
ELECTRA
            …buried lies, bereft
    of grave, or mournful rites from us.

(*Enter* Chrysothemis *running excitedly through a courtyard gate*)

[871]
CHRYSOTHEMIS Rejoice, sister! I've come – with indecent
    haste – to tell you the news! Your troubles have come to
    an end. You need weep no longer!
ELECTRA What makes you think you have found anything
    which could help the misery I feel? There is no cure for
    that.
CHRYSOTHEMIS He's here with us! Orestes! Believe me as
    surely as you can see me!
ELECTRA Have you lost your senses, poor sister? Or do you find
    your present circumstances – and mine – something to
    joke about?
CHRYSOTHEMIS I swear by our ancestral gods, this is no joke.
    He *is* with us.
ELECTRA Oh dear. Where on earth did you hear that? I'm afraid
    you've been completely misled.
CHRYSOTHEMIS I didn't hear it anywhere. I have seen proof
    enough for myself. That is how I know it's true.
ELECTRA What proof? What could you have seen to be so
    ablaze with destructive hope?
CHRYSOTHEMIS By the gods, you must listen! Then, when you
    have heard the rest, say whether I'm telling the truth or
    talking nonsense.

60

ELECTRA All right, say what you have to say, if it makes you feel any better.

CHRYSOTHEMIS So then, I'll tell you all I saw.

As soon as I arrived at the ancestral tomb in which lies our father, I saw streams of fresh milk flowing from the top of the mound, and father's grave was garlanded all round with every kind of flower. I was completely taken aback; then I looked round to make sure no-one else was about. When I saw all was quiet, I crept up to the tomb. There, at the edge of the site of the pyre I saw a freshly cut lock of hair; and immediately an image familiar to my imagination burst upon my poor mind as I realised I was looking at proof of that dearest of men, Orestes.

As I held that lock of hair in my hand, I said nothing to chance fate. My eyes filled with tears of joy! Then as now, I knew that this offering came from no-one else but him. Who could it come from except you or me? I didn't put it there: I know that. Nor did you: how could you? You cannot so much as leave the palace to visit the shrines of the gods without being punished. It would not have entered our mother's head to do it: and I would have known about it if she had.

No; these offerings at the tomb are from Orestes. So take courage, sister. The same demon, which has plagued us so far, will not always threaten you. The past has been hard for us, but today has dawned a brighter day.

ELECTRA How I pity your foolishness.

CHRYSOTHEMIS What's wrong? Are you not pleased at my news?

ELECTRA You have no idea how mistaken you are.

CHRYSOTHEMIS How can I be mistaken about what I saw with my own eyes?

ELECTRA My poor sister, he is dead. The help he might have brought is also dead. Do not look to him.

CHRYSOTHEMIS Oh no. Where did you hear this?

ELECTRA From someone who witnessed his death.

CHRYSOTHEMIS Where is this person? It seems so strange.

ELECTRA In the palace. Our mother finds his news much to her taste.

CHRYSOTHEMIS Oh dear. But who did put the offerings on father's tomb?

ELECTRA They are probably from someone in memory of Orestes, our dead brother.

CHRYSOTHEMIS Poor sister, I hurried here thinking I was bringing happy news. I'd no idea of this latest disaster. And so, I've come here only to find fresh troubles on top of our previous ones.

ELECTRA Such is the case.

But if you do as I say, you can lift our burden of grief.

CHRYSOTHEMIS What am I to do? Raise the dead?

ELECTRA Of course not.

CHRYSOTHEMIS What then?

ELECTRA I have a plan.

CHRYSOTHEMIS I am not against anything that will help.

ELECTRA Remember: there is no success without hardship.

CHRYSOTHEMIS I know. I will do whatever I can.

ELECTRA Listen then.

You fully understand our position – that, of our friends, none is left. Hades has taken them – deprived us of them all; the pair of us are left – alone.

Now, whilst ever I used to hear that our brother was fit and well, I still retained the hope that he would come and avenge father's murder. But now that he is no longer alive, it is to you that I look. You, with me, your sister, must not shrink from killing Aegisthus, our father's murderer.

I can no longer contain my thoughts.

How can you sit idly by? ...clinging to what hope? You *could* simply mourn the loss of your ancestral wealth as you are stripped of it. You *could* suffer in silence for the rest of your life as you grow old, unmarried, with no man to protect you. And don't entertain any false expectations! Aegisthus is not such a fool as to allow you or me to have blossoming families – he knows that would be the end of him.

But if you follow my plans, firstly, you will earn the respect of our dead father and brother in the world below, and secondly, as is your right, you will be called 'free' for the rest of your life, and you will win a marriage worthy of you.

Everyone likes to see true nobility.

As to renown, do you not see how much you will win for yourself and for me if you listen to me? Every citizen and every visitor to our city will be full of praise:

"Look at those two sisters" they will say, "who recovered their family home and risked their lives to kill their powerful enemies. They deserve the love and respect of all of us. At our feasts and at all our gatherings, we should honour them for their courage."

Whether we two live or die, such will be our fame.

Dear sister, listen, work with me for father; toil with me for our brother; relieve me of my pain; put an end to yours; and know this: a shameful life disgraces the well-born.

CHORUS In such circumstances as these, both you that speak and you that listen need to think carefully.

CHRYSOTHEMIS Before you say anything, girls, if she had been sensible and avoided her present difficulties, she would have shown discretion. She has shown none whatsoever.

(*to Electra*) To what purpose do you arm yourself with such boldness and call on me to help? Can you not see? You were born a woman, not a man. You have much less strength in your arm than your enemies have.

Some people have a demon who smiles on them day after day, but ours slips away and does nothing. What woman can plan to overpower such a man and escape unharmed the consequences of her folly?

Now, take care that our present desperate circumstances are not made even more desperate by someone

63

overhearing us. It helps us not at all, having acquired a fine reputation, to die ingloriously. Death is not even the worst that can happen to us: in their hands, we may find ourselves begging for death, but not be able to find it.

I pray of you: before we lose everything and die, and before we ruin our whole family, please, curb your anger. I shall keep what you have said in confidence – as if you had never said it.

Come to your senses; even though it is late in the day, recognize your lack of strength: yield to those in power.

CHORUS Listen to her. Nothing is of greater benefit to man than common sense.

ELECTRA (*to Chrysothemis*) Nothing you say is unexpected. I knew you would throw out everything I suggested. So then, it is left to me, to my hand alone, to do the deed. I make no empty threat.

CHORUS I wish you had had such an attitude at the time of your father's death: you might have prevented all this then.

ELECTRA I had the character – but not the maturity to understand.

CHRYSOTHEMIS You were better without your maturity.

ELECTRA I take it you will not help.

CHRYSOTHEMIS I think, if you try anything, you will fail.

ELECTRA I envy you your mature thinking, but hate your cowardice.

CHRYSOTHEMIS You can criticize or speak well of me as you please.

ELECTRA I certainly shall not be speaking well of you.

CHRYSOTHEMIS You will have plenty of time to think about that.

ELECTRA Go away! You have no helpfulness in you.

CHRYSOTHEMIS I have; but you have no common sense in you.

ELECTRA Go tell all this to your mother!

CHRYSOTHEMIS I don't hate you as much as that!

ELECTRA You should appreciate to what dishonour you are leading me.

CHRYSOTHEMIS Not to dishonour; to common sense.

ELECTRA Am I to follow you to your idea of justice?

CHRYSOTHEMIS When you come to your senses, then you can lead us both there.

ELECTRA A great shame, that you speak so sensibly, but get it so wrong.

CHRYSOTHEMIS You're the one who's getting it wrong.

ELECTRA Are you suggesting I do not have justice on my side?

CHRYSOTHEMIS Unfortunately, it's justice that's doing the damage.

ELECTRA I cannot live by your ethics.

CHRYSOTHEMIS If you did, you would soon thank me.

ELECTRA I won't do anything out of fear for what you have to say.

CHRYSOTHEMIS True. But will you not reconsider?

ELECTRA It's bad advice; there's nothing worse.

CHRYSOTHEMIS You are going to take no notice of what I say anyway.

ELECTRA There's nothing worth taking notice of: you've said it all before.

CHRYSOTHEMIS I'm going now. You don't approve of my advice, nor I of your attitude.

ELECTRA Go indoors then. I shall never follow you ...not even if you wanted me to. Only a fool chases after the pointless.

CHRYSOTHEMIS If that is your idea of common sense, that's fine. But when you come to grief, you will appreciate what I've said.

(*Exit* Chrysothemis *into the palace.*)

SECOND CHORAL SONG

[1058]
CHORUS   *[strophe]*
> When we can see the birds above
> so wisely show such faithfulness
> to parents that them raised
> and ever give delight,
> then why is lack of faith shown here?
> Yet, by the thunderbolt
> of Zeus, by Gods of Right,
> the faithless ones shall not escape.
> Earth's voice, to the dead which speaks,
> now shout in sharp shrill tone
> to Atreus' sons below,
> my joyless sad reproach...

[antistrophe]
> ...reproach that they fare ill abroad
> and that their children's mutual strife
> no longer them allows
> a life with friendship blest.
> Alone, betrayed, now in distress,
> Electra sadly mourns
> all that has gone before; and
> as the all-lamenting nightingale,
> she has no heed of death
> but, ready for her doom,
> her twofold Furies smites.
> Who now, well-born, so lives?

None counted 'mongst the good
will badly live, or foolishly
good reputation lose.
But you have chosen a life
of lamentation pure,
to win from what is base
the prize of double gain:
the name of wise and noble child.

[antistrophe]

So may you live in wealth
so far above your enemies
as now you live beneath,
since you devoid I find
of honourable share;
but what is best is now
your right, so nobly won
by offering Zeus your piety.

THIRD EPISODE

(*Enter* Orestes *and* Retinue, *one of whom carries a bronze urn,
through a courtyard gate*)

[1098]
ORESTES Girls, can you tell us if we have heard aright – that this
     is the place we're looking for?
CHORUS Where do you want to be?
ORESTES Aegisthus ... Is this where he lives?
CHORUS Yes, this is the place.
ORESTES Which one of you is going to go in and say I would
     like to meet him?
CHORUS (*indicating Electra*) She will. She is best placed.
ORESTES Girl; go in and tell Aegisthus that some men have
     journeyed here from Phocia to see him.

ELECTRA Oh dear. Are you bringing proof of the reports we
    have heard?
ORESTES I don't know if it is any of your business, but an old
    man, Strophius, has sent me with news of Orestes.
ELECTRA Tell *me* the news, please!
    How afraid I feel!
ORESTES To put it simply, we bring his remains, as you can see.
    He is dead.
ELECTRA Oh no! Your news is clear! I see it for certain.
ORESTES If it is for Orestes you weep, this urn indeed houses
    what is left of his body.
ELECTRA Stranger, if that is so, please let me hold the urn in my
    hands. I shall weep over those ashes as I lament my own
    fate and that of my whole family.
ORESTES (*to Retinue*) Let her hold the urn. Whoever she is, she
    bears no ill-will: she speaks as a friend, perhaps a family
    member.

(*Member of Retinue gives Electra the urn*)

ELECTRA All that is left as a memorial to the soul of the man
    who was dearest to me, Orestes... How far distant from
    the hopes I had when I sent you away, I now receive you
    back.
    Now mere nothingness, I hold you in my hands; how
    bright-eyed when I sent you from home.
    I ought, indeed, to have quitted this life before I ever sent
    you away to a foreign home, as, with these same hands, I
    secreted you away to avoid your murder, only for you to
    rest here in death today as you wait to receive your
    allotted place in your ancestral tomb.
    Away from home, an exile in some foreign land, you met
    an evil death, separated from your sister. I did not take
    you in my loving arms and prepare your body for the
    funeral rites, nor did I lift your sorry remains from the
    burnt-out pyre. But, poor man, you were tended by the

68

hands of strangers and come to me as a small pile of ash in this small urn.

To think of the pointlessness of that sweet duty I used to perform when, in times past, I looked after you! You were never your mother's dear one more than mine. Those who lived here were not the ones to look after you; it was I that was your nurse, even though you always called me 'sister'.

All this has gone in a single day, with news of your death. You have left us, and in so doing, you have destroyed everything – and with storm-like vehemence. Father has passed away; I am as good as dead, and you, in death, are no longer with us. And our enemies are laughing. My mother, who is no mother, is delirious with pleasure; you often used to send me secret messages about her: that you would come yourself to exact revenge. But your evil demon, and mine, has snatched all that away and has sent you to me, not in the form that I would dearly have wanted, but as useless ash.

O pitiable body... On what a dreadful journey, my dearest, you were sent here... And you have destroyed me. Yes, you have destroyed me, my dearest brother.

Take me inside your urn, as nothingness to be with nothingness, to dwell with you below for ever. I shared everything with you equally whilst you were on Earth; and now I want to die and never to leave your tomb. For, I see no grief amongst the dead.

CHORUS   Remember, Electra, you were born of mortal father; Orestes too was mortal. Do not be over-wrought. It is due to us all to suffer the same fate.

ORESTES   Oh, what shall I say? What sentiments am I trying to express? I seem to have lost the power of speech.

ELECTRA   Whatever is the matter?

ORESTES   Are you Electra?

ELECTRA   I am; and in a sorry state.

ORESTES   Oh, no!

ELECTRA   But, stranger, you are surely not concerned about me?

ORESTES So dishonourably and impiously abused…

ELECTRA You certainly well describe my misfortune.

ORESTES I pity your life, ill-fated and unmarried.

ELECTRA Why, stranger, do you gaze at me and why are you so concerned?

ORESTES I understood nothing of the enormity of what I face.

ELECTRA Why? What has been said?

ORESTES I can see you are consumed with pain.

ELECTRA And yet you have seen only a small portion of my misery.

ORESTES How could it be any worse?

ELECTRA Because I have to live with the murderers.

ORESTES Murderers?

ELECTRA My father's. And I live here under duress as their slave.

ORESTES Who compels you?

ELECTRA She is called my mother, although she does not behave as such.

ORESTES How does she behave? Is she violent or does she deprive you in some way?

ELECTRA …violence, deprivation, every form of maltreatment…

ORESTES Is there no-one here to help you, to put an end to this?

ELECTRA There was someone; but you have now brought me his ashes.

ORESTES Ill-fated girl! As I look on you, how sorry for you I feel.

ELECTRA You are the only one who does.

ORESTES I am the only one who comes to help you.

ELECTRA Are you a relation from somewhere?

ORESTES I would tell you, but (*indicating Chorus*) are they well-disposed to us?

ELECTRA Yes, you may speak in front of them.

ORESTES Let go of that urn; and I will tell you everything.

ELECTRA By the gods, don't make me do that!

ORESTES You can trust me.

ELECTRA (*falls to her knees*) Do not take what is dearest from me!

70

ORESTES I said I would help.

ELECTRA (*clinging hold of the urn*) Orestes, I could not bear it
     if I were parted from you!

ORESTES Speak auspiciously! It is not right for you to weep.

ELECTRA How can it not be right to weep for a dead brother?

ORESTES You should not say such things.

ELECTRA I am to dishonour the dead?

ORESTES You dishonour no-one. That is not what you are doing.

ELECTRA No, so long as I hold this body of Orestes.

ORESTES That is not Orestes. That was simply a story.

ELECTRA Then where is his grave?

ORESTES There is none. The living do not have a grave.

ELECTRA What is that you say?

ORESTES I would not lie...

ELECTRA Does he live?

ORESTES As I do.

ELECTRA Are you he?

ORESTES (*showing Electra a signet ring he is wearing*) See my
     father's seal, and know that I tell the truth.

ELECTRA My dearest!

ORESTES Yes; my dearest one!

ELECTRA Have you really come?

ORESTES You may be certain of that.

ELECTRA I have you in my arms?

ORESTES As you will for ever.

ELECTRA Girls! Everyone! See, Orestes is here! He feigned his
     death and now, by feigning, is safe returned.

CHORUS We see him child; and now our tears are tears of joy.

[Recitative with musical accompaniment]

[1232]
ELECTRA   *[strophe]*
    Son of him
    most dear to me of anyone!
    At last you've come;
    You've found us, reached us, looked on us!
ORESTES
    Yes we are here; but say naught yet.
ELECTRA
    Why say you that?
ORESTES
    Silence, lest any inside hear.
ELECTRA
    By the unchained goddess
    Artemis,
    we should not tremble in fear
    at that so odd-made mass
    of womanhood inside!
ORESTES
    In women, Ares god of war
    lives oft; you know that for yourself.
ELECTRA
    aiaíaiaí!
    You mention evils unresolved
    which me beset as clear as day
    and which I'll not forget.
ORESTES
    I know. And when free speech is ours,
    then only, deeds as these recall.

ELECTRA   *[antistrophe]*
    All of time
    is needed now for me to say
    all that I would;
    For, scarcely can I check my words!
ORESTES
    I feel the same; but talk not now.
ELECTRA
    And our intent…?
ORESTES
    …does not allow of lengthy speech.
ELECTRA
    But who would, now that
    you are here,
    silence for words exchange,
    since unexpected and
    unhoped for, you I see?
ORESTES
    You see me at the time the gods
    prescribed for me to come back home.
ELECTRA
    A greater boon
    than former grace, if you a god
    to these our halls has brought. Of gods
    this is I think the work.
ORESTES
    I shrink to curb rejoicing now,
    but fear lest pleasure overwhelms.

ELECTRA   *[epode]*
    So long a time…;
    the dearest journey now you've made
    to come before me thus.
    You see me stricken; hence…
ORESTES
    Hence what should I…?

73

ELECTRA

    ...do not deprive me of

    the pleasure of your face.

ORESTES

    My anger would on others bear.

ELECTRA

    Agree to my request...

ORESTES

                ...How not?

ELECTRA

    My dear, all hope I'd lost to hear

    your voice. My speechless anger checked,

    I listened, wretched, cries suppressed.

    But now I have you; you are here,

    the dearest sight,

    forgotten not, 'spite all my ills.

[End of recitative]

[1288]

ORESTES I want no superfluous information. I need no lessons about how evil our mother is nor how Aegisthus squanders our family possessions – how he grossly overspends here or is wildly extravagant there. The list would be far too long for the time we have.

So, tell me what I need to know right now: where to confront them or, indeed, where to conceal ourselves, so that we can put an end to our enemies' merrymaking.

To begin with, you need to make sure that our mother does not see your happy face and realise that we are at her door: you must continue to mourn my pretended fate. When we have success, that will be the time to rejoice and laugh freely.

ELECTRA Brother, I will do as you say: you wish is mine too, since I have no pleasure but that which I take from you, and I would do nothing on my own account if it meant

74

hurting you even a little: that would not be serving the god who is looking after us.

But, you know how matters stand, of course. You have heard that Aegisthus is not at home, whilst mother is inside. And have no fear that she might see me with a happy radiant face. An ancient hatred has sunk deep into me and since I have seen you, I shall never stop weeping *for joy*. How could I, seeing you in one moment both dead and alive? For me, you have achieved the impossible; so much so that if father were to appear alive before me, I would not think him a ghost, but would believe him real.

Now that you have made your journey to be with us, begin as your spirit urges, and know that I, by myself, would not have failed on both of two counts: either I would have saved myself nobly, or nobly I would have died.

ORESTES Be quiet now; I hear someone coming out.

ELECTRA   And you must all go in, and give those inside something they cannot refuse – or enjoy!

(*Enter* Pedagogue *from the palace*)

[1326]

PEDAGOGUE   You fools! Do you care nothing for your lives? Were you born with no sense? Don't you realise the great danger you are in? If I hadn't kept guard here by the door, your intensions would have been inside the Hall before you were! Fortunately *I* have shown some diligence. So put an end to your conversation and your laughing and singing! This is no time for delay: it is time to act!

ORESTES I'm about to go in. How are things inside?

PEDAGOGUE They are fine. No-one knows who you are.

ORESTES You have told them I am dead?

PEDAGOGUE You are in Hades.

ORESTES Are they pleased? What do they say?

PEDAGOGUE I will tell you when this is over. As it now stands, everything is well, including what is not well.

ELECTRA Who is this, brother?

75

ORESTES Do you not know?

ELECTRA No; tell me.

ORESTES Do you not remember to whom you gave me as a
child?

ELECTRA What are you saying?

ORESTES …into whose arms you carefully entrusted me when I
was smuggled away to Phocia?

ELECTRA Is he the one trustworthy man I found at the time of
father's murder?

ORESTES He is. But that's enough.

ELECTRA O dearest man, the sole saviour of the house of
Agamemnon! How are you?

Are you really he who saved Orestes and me in our time
of trouble? You are the dearest of men, who performed the
sweetest of services. How could you be with us so long
without my realising it and without your giving any sign?
Rather you nearly killed me with your words even though
your deeds were sweet.

Rejoice, father: yes; I see you as a father! And know how
much I both hated and loved you in one day!

PEDAGOGUE Enough of this! It will take many days and nights
to tell you the whole story, Electra.

And to you two, I say now is the time to act! Clytemnestra
is alone. None of the men are inside. If you delay, you will
regret it when you find yourselves in a fight with others
more skilful and numerous than anyone in there now!

ORESTES No more talk then; Pylades, let us enter quickly – as
soon as we have done reverence to our ancestral gods that
dwell in the entrance.

(*Orestes, Pedagogue and Retinue kneel to the statues of the gods
in the entrance to the Great Hall; then:*
Exeunt Orestes, Pylades, Pedagogue *and* Retinue *into the Great
Hall.*)

ELECTRA Lord Apollo, hear graciously my prayer both for them and for me who have made many offerings to you with a suppliant's hand.

But now, O Apollo Lyceüs, with whatever I have, I beg and fall before you with my prayer that you should favour us with your help in our present undertaking, and show to mankind the reward for impiety meted out by the gods!

THIRD CHORAL SONG

[1384]
CHORUS   *[strophe]*

See advancing,
Ares breathing blood unfailing.
None escapes the hounds of vengeance
entering now the palace doors,
vengeance seeking 'gainst the wicked.
Soon will they the dream fulfil.

                              [antistrophe]

From the dead, now
stealthy-footed help has reached a
father's home of ancient riches,
bearing keen-edged blooded death.
Hermes leads them; darkness hides them.
None can stop them reach their goal.

CONCLUSION

[Recitative with musical accompaniment]

[1398]
ELECTRA   *[strophe]*
 My dearest friends, the men will soon
 the deed complete. So wait. Say naught.
CHORUS
 What *are* they doing?…
ELECTRA
     …*She* an urn
 prepares for burial; *they* stand near.

(*Electra looks out through the courtyard gates*)

CHORUS
 What look you for?...
ELECTRA
     …I watch for fear
 Aegisthus home returns unseen.
CLYTEMNESTRA (*from inside the palace; screaming*)
 Aiaíaiaí!!
 O friendless house with murderers filled!!
ELECTRA
 But someone screams! Hear that, my friends?
CHORUS
 We heard, distraught, such sounds
 as make us shudder.
CLYTEMNESTRA
 Aegisthus! No! Where are you now?
ELECTRA
 And someone cries again!...
CLYTEMNESTRA
   …My child!
 Your mother pity, child!...

78

ELECTRA
>...You gave
>not him nor father pity once!

CHORUS
>O city lost; O wretched race!
>Your fortune day by day does die.

CLTEMNESTRA
>I'm stabbed!...

ELECTRA
>...Again!!...and twice as hard!

CLYTEMNESTRA
>No No!!...

ELECTRA
>...And where's Aegisthus now?`

CHORUS
>The curse complete. They live,
>who lie beneath the earth.
>The dead, in vengeance, have destroyed
>the blood of killers.

(Enter Orestes *and* Pylades *from the Great Hall: Orestes' knife is covered in blood. They stand in the entrance.*)

[1422]
CHORUS   *[antistrophe]*
>Here blood-red hands with sacrifice
>to Ares drip; we blame them not.

ELECTRA
>Orestes, fared you well?...

ORESTES
>...Yes, well,
>if well Apollo us advised.

ELECTRA
>Is *she* now dead, the wretch?...

ORESTES

    …No more
will mother's arrogance abuse.

ELECTRA

    O noble day,
    that sees the end of torment all…

ORESTES

    …and welcomes in our life anew!

CHORUS

    But stop. I see Aegis-
    -thus now approaching.

ORESTES

    We thought that he would be away.

ELECTRA

    But now returns?...

ORESTES

    …Yes, you can see:
    the man is in our power…

ELECTRA

    …Good!
    So happily he comes from town.

CHORUS (*to Orestes and Pylades*)

    Behind the doors now quickly go!
    Success so far! Now finish well!

ORESTES

    Be brave. We'll do it…

ELECTRA

    …Yes, press on.

(*Orestes, and Pylades go through the doors of the Great Hall, where they keep out of sight of Aegisthus*)

ORESTES

    We're set…

(*The doors of the Great Hall close*)

ELECTRA
                    ...Next, *I* must play my part.
CHORUS
        Perhaps to say some words
        of gentle nature now
        would benefit, as hastens he
        to hidden justice.

(*Enter* Aegisthus *through a courtyard gate*)

[1442]

AEGISTHUS   Do any of you know the whereabouts of the
        Phocians? They say they have news that Orestes has been
        killed in a chariot race.
        (*to Electra*) I'm speaking to you! Yes you! You who have
        been so insolent of late! This is of particular interest to
        you and so you in particular will know about it.
ELECTRA   Of course I know about it. How could I not? I am no
        stranger to the death of my loved ones.
AEGISTHUS   So where are these Phocians then. Come on; tell
        me.
ELECTRA   They are inside. They have already met their hostess.
AEGISTHUS   Have they really brought news of his death?
ELECTRA   No... they have brought proof, not merely news.
AEGISTHUS   Are there some means by which we can be certain
        then?
ELECTRA   They present indeed an unenviable sight.
AEGISTHUS   You say much to cheer me, which is unusual for
        you.
ELECTRA   Rejoice to your heart's content, if you have anything
        to rejoice at.
AEGISTHUS   I now order you to be silent and to open up the
        gates so that all the citizens of Mycenae and Argos may
        see his corpse; and if any of them nurtured empty hopes of
        him, let them now accept the bit and not strain against my
        correction!

ELECTRA All is at an end. For after so long a time, I finally see
    the sense of making peace with the stronger.

(*The doors of the Great Hall open to reveal the completely
shrouded body of Clytemnestra.*
Orestes *and* Retinue *are standing behind the body.*
Enter Orestes *and* Retinue *so as to prevent Aegisthus escaping
through the courtyard gates.*)

[1466]
AEGISTHUS O Zeus, I see the form of a man whose death, if I
    may be so bold as to say so, has arisen not without the
    malice of the gods.
    Pull back the shroud which covers his face – so that, as a
    kinsman, he may be mourned by me also.
ORESTES *You* should lift up the shroud. It is for you, not me, to
    look on it – and say some kindly words.
AEGISTHUS You are right; I should.
    (*to Electra*) You; if Clytemnestra is at home, call her here.
ORESTES She is by you. You need look no further.

(*Aegisthus pulls back the shroud, and recoils*)

AEGISTHUS Ah! What is this I see?
ORESTES You seem fearful? Do you not recognize …someone?
AEGISTHUS What men are you into whose nets I have fallen?
ORESTES Have you not yet realised that you speak to one who is
    alive not dead?
AEGISTHUS I understand. You are presumably none other than
    Orestes.

(*Orestes draws his knife*)

ORESTES Such a man of perception to have been deceived
    before.
AEGISTHUS My death is near. But let me say something…

82

ELECTRA Let him say nothing! By the gods, brother, no lengthy words!
          What does a mortal man, imbued with evil and about to die, gain from delay?
          Kill him quickly, and when you have killed him, feed his body to the grave-diggers he deserves, out of our sight.
          This is the only deliverance I could ever have from the evils of the past.
ORESTES (*to Aegisthus*) Go inside. The issue now is not of words but of your soul.
AEGISTHUS Why do you take me inside. If your action is good, why do you need the cover of darkness? And why are you not ready to kill me?
ORESTES Give me no orders. Go inside to the place where you killed my father. You will die at the same spot.
AEGISTHUS Does the house of Pelops really need to see its curse continue now and into the future, with death upon death?
ORESTES *Your* death in fact. I can prophecy that accurately.
AEGISTHUS Not an inherited skill, in your case...
ORESTES You've too much to say. No more delay: move on, inside.
AEGISTHUS Lead the way...
ORESTES You go first...
AEGISTHUS ...surely you're not afraid I'll escape?
ORESTES You will make no choices about your death, which I will ensure is bitter. And I must now apply this universal justice: to put to death any who wish to act beyond the law. Otherwise, villainy would be of no account.

(*Exeunt* Aegisthus *and* Orestes *into the Great Hall*)

CHORUS
          Seed of Atreus, so much suffered,
          you have won your hard-fought freedom,
          firmly, by these deeds, established.